The Root of All Evil

By Illiad

O'REILLY®

Beijing · Cambridge · Farnham · Köln · Paris · Sebastopol · Taipei · Tokyo

The Root of All Evil
by Illiad

Printed in the United States of America.

Editor: Troy Mott
Production Editor: Catherine Morris
Cover Designer: Ellie Volckhausen
Interior Designers: David Futato and Melanie Wang

Printing History:
August 2001:   First Edition.

ISBN: 0-596-00193-2
[M]

To my li'l buddy Champ,
who never caused me any sorrow
until the day he had to go away.

Other books by Illiad:

User Friendly: The Comic Strip
Evil Geniuses in a Nutshell: A User Friendly Guide to World Domination

ACKNOWLEDGMENTS

As the list of people I feel I owe grows longer, I find that I have to in some way keep it under control. It's kind of like getting wildly wealthier, except you can't exchange a person for a banana daiquiri. At least, not in this country.

For their support of U.F. and their outstanding professionalism, the entire gang at O'Reilly. Including Tim. Tim has chutzpah.

Eric Raymond and Alan Cox, for their superlative contributions to my mad universe.

Kethy, Stephanie, and Big Mike, you guys helped more than you know.

For their faith, talent, and inexorable drive to succeed, Erik, Graham, Jaleen, Erin, Greg, Reg, Christian, Jay and Debra.

Barry, Davey, Laura Jo, and Jas, for holding the ship steady as I slide all over the deck.

Every UFie, everywhere, for ultimately making all of this possible.

Sharon, for musing when I'm museless.

Tom, Ken, Toomas, and Steven, because you guys STILL crack me up.

Valaria, for being tiny.

Geoff, for teaching me how to speak like a "Souf Effrican."

And finally, for having been there from the beginning and lending a hand or shoulder whenever I asked, Natalie, Alan, and Dana.

If I forgot to mention you, please forgive me and let me buy you that banana daiquiri.

COLOPHON

The cover illustration for *The Root of All Evil* was provided by Illiad. The cover was designed by Ellie Volckhausen and produced by Emma Colby using QuarkXPress 4.1. David Futato and Melanie Wang designed and produced the interior layout using QuarkXPress 4.1 and the Monotype Gill Sans font. Alex Russell prepared the illustrations for print using Photoshop 5.5. Catherine Morris was the production editor. Claire Cloutier, Catherine Morris, David Futato, and Hanna Dyer provided quality control.

A NEEDLESS INTRODUCTION

User Friendly readers need an introduction to a new volume the way L.A. Lakers fans need an announcer to introduce Kobe Bryant. Anyone who has read one of the previous volumes or followed the exploits of the Dust Puppy and his Evil Genius associates at *www.userfriendly.org* already knows what to expect: a look into a mad world.

The interesting part is that while it's mad all right, most of it isn't made up. I haven't yet run into a talking Dust Puppy with feet, but there are precious few characters in the User Friendly universe that I haven't met. The situations are real, too. The perpetual mutual incomprehension between the techies and the marketing guys. The inability of the techies to understand even each other. OS wars, and version feuds, and the need to forget even important differences like Mandrake vs. Slackware to present a solid front when faced by The Evil Empire: it's all in here, and it's all out there in the real world, too.

And that's probably the only reason other than tradition for there to be an introduction: to tell those unfortunates who don't already know about User Friendly and the Evil Geniuses that they have in store for them not just a treat but an education.

Now for those who haven't the faintest notion of what I am talking about: you need this book more than the rest of us. They're out there. They are building the world you live in, and you haven't the faintest notion of what they are doing, and you won't until suddenly you are faced with its consequences. Think the computer world intrudes into your space now? Think it's incomprehensible now? You ain't seen nothing yet.

It's coming like Lucifer's Hammer, folks, and you better learn about it, and while there are serious works on the computer revolution and its consequences they tend to be dry and unreadable. So where do you go to change your mindset and get a little insight into the Evil Geniuses who even now remake your world into something that you never asked for and may not like?

Right here.

And that's the real secret: it's all real. I haven't met him yet, but I wouldn't be astonished to find that the Dust Puppy has been drawn from a real-life creature. Certainly Greg and Miranda and A.J., who can't even talk to a techie girl without using a keyboard and smilies and stuff, have been. You can meet The Smiling Man in any corporate headquarters, and he's a lot closer to real life than that pointy-headed goon.

So: if you're wired into this weird world that lurks out there, the irreducible minimum that lives on dot weal or dot woe, you already know about User Friendly and you're only reading this to see if I make a mistake so you can send me a gloating email; and if you aren't and you haven't a clue as to what I am talking about, for heaven's sake buy this book and its predecessors and find out before it's too late!

Jerry Pournelle
Hollywood, California
June 2001

A WORD FROM THE AUTHOR

Well, a few hundred words, really.

Lately, a lot of people have been asking me about the future of content on the Internet. Since I've had very little experience as a seer, I'd normally resort to the magic eight-ball for an answer. But online content is something I'm passionate about—passionate enough, in fact, to go out on a limb and let people know what it is I think will come about.

When you're plugged right in to an outspoken audience—and this is something you can't avoid unless you sequester yourself in an ivory tower—it's easy to sense changes. Changes in attitude, changes in expectations, even changes in the constituency of the readership. We all know that people resist and dread change, because change introduces uncertainty. Much better to remain in the secure, safe world of the known than to step forward into a strange light, no matter how bright it is.

I do sense a change coming, and a fairly major one at that. It won't be sudden, I don't think. Rather, we'll see a gradual shifting in attitude and acceptance. The pendulum that swung to one extreme with the vast monies poured into companies with no business model has swung to the other extreme, where advertisers and investment firms measure dollars spent against a very harsh performance yardstick, one that has never been utilized in the offline world. The change we're going to see is the pendulum swinging back into the middle.

The extremes are places where ideas and concepts are fattened then reduced in a crucible. When you get to the middle, that's where you see steady, real growth. And that's where online content is headed.

I've always been a believer in the Internet as a means of getting around the "popularity middleman." Soon, no longer will the recording artist or cartoonist (among others) have to sell themselves to a traditional record label or a syndicate first to establish credibility. Rather, they can go directly to the audience, the people who should be making the decisions as to what is popular and what isn't. Once that acceptance is in place, you, as a creator, bring in a savvy business unit to help you extend your reach. It's already happening; this book, the third in the series, is proof positive.

Making money from online content has always been a quandary. Apart from porn and gambling sites, historically, content sites have had poor results in generating subscription income, mostly because just about everything was FREE when the Web exploded, and that set a powerful precedent. Then the bottom dropped out of online advertising, crippling many sites and utterly demolishing others. But again, a change is coming about. Soon, I think you'll see choices on content sites, where you can still get your content for free, or you can pay a fee and do away with advertising and other promotional gimmicks. At the same time, online advertising will re-establish itself as being effective, and at reasonable rates. It's all about finding the groove in the middle of the road.

I'm certain that online content will get there. It won't vanish anytime soon, because the audiences are here to stay. And as long as the audience is there, creators like myself will want to keep creating.

J.D. Frazer

POST Y2K GARAGE SALES

EXPLAINING THE CSS-DECRYPTION SOURCE CODE TO THE MOTION PICTURE ASSOCIATION OF AMERICA

A RECENT ADDITION IS UNVEILED ON A CERTAIN ORGANIZATION CHART

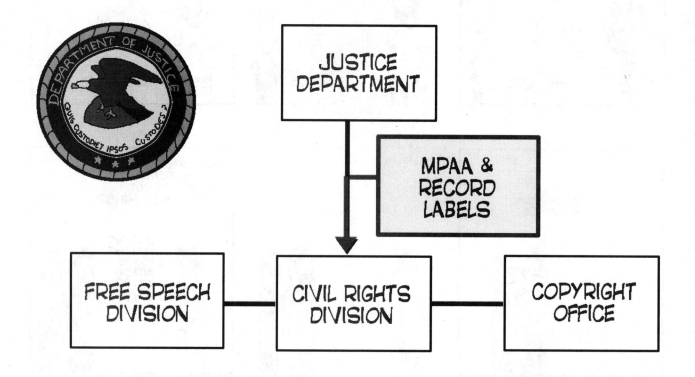

HEY, I JUST HEARD THAT PITR GOT ARRESTED FOR ASSAULT. HE'S IN JAIL RIGHT NOW.

HE'S IN JAIL?

YEAH. HE PHONED AND SOUNDED REALLY DEPRESSED. SAID SOMETHING ABOUT EVEN THE POLICE BEING "A PART OF THEM."

WE ARE ALL DOOMED.

HEY HEY! YOU GOT BAIL!

TECH SUPPORT. GREG SPEAKING.

HELLO. MY COMPUTER SCREEN WENT ALL BLUE ON ME AND I DON'T LIKE IT.

WELL I CAN'T SAY I BLAME YOU. YOU JUST SUFFERED THE BLUE SCREEN OF DEATH. A FATAL ERROR UNDER WINDOWS.

YOU'RE TELLING ME. BLUE LOOKS JUST HIDEOUS WITH A BEIGE FRAME. HOW DO I CHANGE IT TO A PRETTIER COLOUR?

DO YOU LIKE BLACK? MOVE THE POWER SWITCH TO "OFF."

YOU DON'T LOOK ALL THAT HAPPY TODAY MIRANDA. DIDN'T YOU GET A VALENTINES?

NO, I DIDN'T. BUT THAT'S NOT THE POINT.

I'M JUST TIRED OF SEEING VALENTINES BEING GIVEN BY PEOPLE WHO JUST WANT TO GET INTO YOUR PANTS. I MEAN, WHATEVER HAPPENED TO GIVING OUT OF DEEP FRIENDSHIP?

OH MIRANDA. I'M SURE IT'S HAPPENING SOMEWHERE.

SORRY FOR ALWAYS YANKING THE BALL AWAY, CHARLES.

THAT'S OKAY. IT'S NOT LIKE I NEVER EXPECTED IT.

MORAL: READ THE FINE PRINT ON ALL CERTIFICATIONS.

19

SPECULATION ON THE D.O.J. RECOMMENDATIONS TO **BREAK MICROSOFT APART** CONTINUE THIS WEEK AS ANALYSTS EVALUATE THE CONSEQUENCES OF THE ANTI-TRUST TRIAL DECISION.

WHEN ASKED TO OFFER A LIKELY RESULT OF THE BREAKUP. ONE ANALYST STATED THAT SHE COULD SEE THE SOFTWARE GIANT SPLIT INTO **THREE COMPANIES.**

"OPERATING SYSTEM, APPLICATIONS AND INTERNET?" WE ASKED.

"SALES, MARKETING AND LEGAL." SHE REPLIED.

TECH SUPPORT. GREG SPEAKING.

QUICK! HOW DO I CHANGE MY WALLPAPER?

WELL IT'S PRETTY EASY. I ASSUME YOU WANT TO CHANGE THE APPEARANCE OF YOUR DESKTOP?

I NEED TO GET A PICTURE OFF MY BACKGROUND!

OH I SEE... DID SOMEONE ACCIDENTALLY SET A **PORN PICTURE** AS THEIR WALLPAPER. AND THEIR **WIFE** OR **MOM** IS ABOUT TO SHOW UP?

PLEASE **HURRY!**

HEY TANYA? WHERE HAVE STEF AND A.J. BEEN? I HAVEN'T SEEN THEM FOR A FEW DAYS.

THEY LEFT FOR THAT **CeBIT** COMPUTER SHOW IN GERMANY.

GERMANY? THOSE TWO? NEITHER OF THEM SPEAKS A WORD OF GERMAN!

OH DON'T WORRY. I'M SURE THEY'LL LEARN THE MOST IMPORTANT PHRASES.

STEF, TRY **ANYTHING!** IT'S BEEN **THREE DAYS!**

TOILETZEN! ERR... WASHROOMSTEIN! **TINKLEPLATZ!**

TWITS.

PATENTLY RIDICULOUS

US71034544:
Patent for the letter "a"

US71034545:
Patent for using the letter "a" twice in one word

US71034550:
Patent for the colour "orange"

US71034553:
Patent for a graphic of a smile

US71034571:
Patent for the use of drop shadows in logos

US71034572:
Patent for the "dot" in "dot com"

US71034579:
May as well patent the "com" part as well

THE TRUTH BEHIND THE
DISAPPEARANCE OF GNUTELLA

36

AND TWO BABIES MAKE FOUR

PITR, AM THINKINK YOU ARE TRYINK TO BE GETTINK ME IN BIK TROUBLE...

AM APPRECIATINK YOUR ATTEMPTS - BIKINI MODELS ON MY WALLPAPER, ILLEGAL COPY OF PHOTOSHOP IN MY DESK, OFFICE SUPPLIES IN TRUNK OF CAR...

...BUT, THE BLUE DRESS WITH STAIN IN CLOSET WAS A BIT MUCH, NYET?

WAS ONLY SOY SAUCE.

INCRIMINATING EVIDENCE:
'DARK SIDE' DAVE REVEALS HIS SQUISHY SIDE

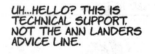

42

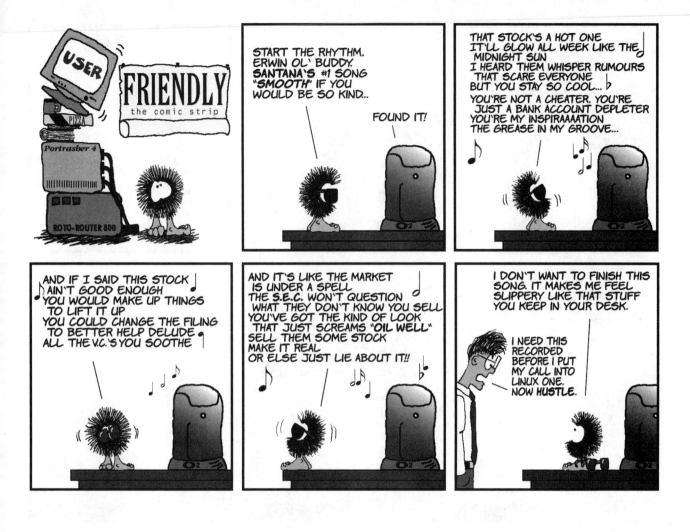

"A BEAR WITH VERY LITTLE BRAIN"

THOSE WACKY EGYPTIANS

52

ONE OF THESE THINGS
IS NOT LIKE THE OTHERS...

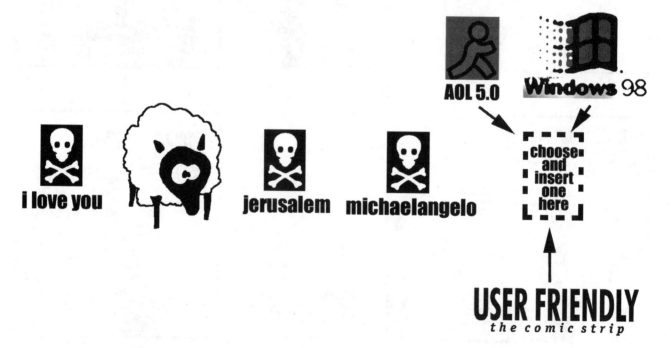

NOW THAT THINGS HAVE SETTLED DOWN A LITTLE WITH THIS NAPSTER THING I CAN START SURFING FOR SOME TUNES...

WHAT YOU'RE DOING IS UNETHICAL. FOR EVERY SONG YOU DOWNLOAD, YOU'RE DEPRIVING AN ARTIST OF MONEY THAT COULD KEEP THEM FROM STARVING.

DOWNLOADING "DA DOO RON RON" BY SHAUN CASSIDY

THEY ALSO GET ALL OF THE CHICKS. I FIGURE THEY OWE ME.

YOU'RE GOOD. WANT TO WORK FOR THE RIAA?

LOOK. I WORK FOR METALLICA. MOVE ASIDE. I HAVE WORK TO DO HERE.

OH PLEASE. YOU HARDLY INSPIRE FEAR.

WHAM!
WHAM!
WHAM!
WHAM!
WHAM!
WHAM!

YE GODS. AND YOU'RE FROM METALLICA'S LEGAL DEPARTMENT?

HELL NO. PUBLIC RELATIONS.

WHERE IS EVERYONE TODAY? THERE'S NOT A TECH IN SIGHT. THEY'D BETTER NOT BE GOOFING OFF...

HI CHIEF! WANT TO SEE THE NEW DATAFLIPBIT-O-TRON WE INSTALLED THIS MORNING?

OH THERE YOU ALL ARE. HA HA. NO NO. YOU TECHS JUST CARRY ON.

OKAY. HE'S GONE.

PLAY THE LORD OF THE RINGS MOVIE TRAILER AGAIN. I WANT TO SEE LIV TYLER BOUNCING ON THAT HORSE.

LIV SHMIV. SHE HAS THICK ANKLES.

THE LAST TIME THE GOVERNMENT DECIDED WE NEEDED A MAJOR SPLIT IN A HURRY...

The MANHATTAN PROJECT
1945

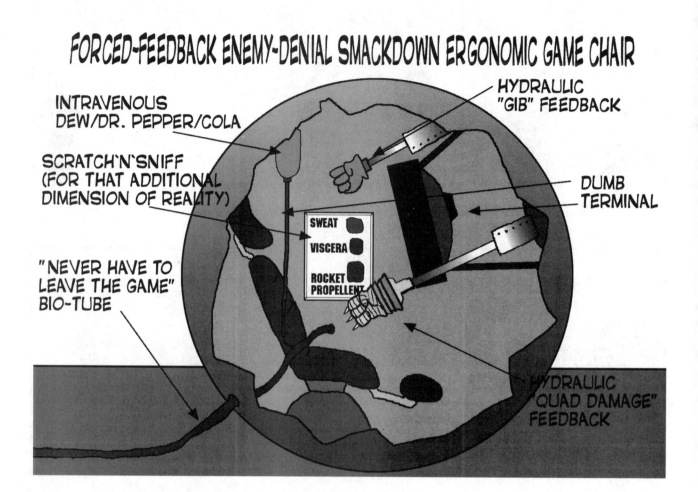

FORCED-FEEDBACK ENEMY-DENIAL SMACKDOWN ERGONOMIC GAME CHAIR

HYDRAULIC "GIB" FEEDBACK

INTRAVENOUS DEW/DR. PEPPER/COLA

SCRATCH`N`SNIFF (FOR THAT ADDITIONAL DIMENSION OF REALITY)

DUMB TERMINAL

SWEAT

VISCERA

ROCKET PROPELLENT

"NEVER HAVE TO LEAVE THE GAME" BIO-TUBE

HYDRAULIC "QUAD DAMAGE" FEEDBACK

STEF BOUGHT A **WHAT?**

AN "ERGONOMIC GAME ENVIRON." THEY CALL IT A **CHAIR** IF YOU CAN BELIEVE IT.

HE'S IN THERE NOW?

OH YAH.

BROMP! BLAMM! BLAMM! SPLOOTC CRUMP!

HE'S PLAYING QUAKE IN THERE?

NO. "LEATHER GODDESSES OF PHOBOS."

DON'T ASK ME HOW BUT I FEEL...MOIST.

Panel 1:
YOU WANTED TO SEE ME, CHIEF?

YES, MIRANDA. I'VE BEEN GIVING CONSIDERATION TO THE IDEA OF HIRING A TECHNICAL MANAGER. SO OF COURSE I WANT TO GIVE ALL OF THE TECHS HERE A CHANCE TO COMPETE FOR THE POSITION.

Panel 2:
AND THESE DAYS I'D HATE TO BE ACCUSED OF NOT BEING AWARE OF THE DEARTH OF WOMEN IN SENIOR TECHNICAL POSITIONS. BUT ON THE **SAME** NOTE, I DO NEED JUSTIFICATION FOR GIVING YOU THE JOB JUST BECAUSE YOU **ARE** A WOMAN...

Panel 3:
ALL OF MY QUALIFICATIONS **ASIDE**, YOU **COULD** ARGUE THAT WOMEN MAKE BETTER **TECHNICAL MANAGERS** BECAUSE WE KNOW HOW TO HANDLE LARGE GROUPS OF **CHILDREN**.

THE JOB IS YOURS. PITR'S FEEDING IS IN TWO HOURS.

Panel 4:
HEY, I HEARD YOU'RE OUR TECH MANAGER NOW. CONGRATS.

I'M NOT SURE I SHOULD BE ALL THAT HAPPY ABOUT IT.

Panel 5:
GUESS YOU HEARD ABOUT HAVING TO FEED PITR?

WHAT **IS** THAT ABOUT?

Panel 6:
YOU'LL MAKE A.J. HAPPY. HE DREW THE SHORT STRAW THIS MORNING.

WHAT AM I DELIVERING TO PITR TODAY? PIZZA?

Panel 7:

SEE, PITR'S BEEN SEQUESTERED IN THAT OFFICE 24 HOURS A DAY FOR THE PAST WEEK WORKING ON ACCOUNTING CODE. IT'S A CRUNCH PERIOD AND HE'S UNDER THE GUN SO WE TAKE TURNS DELIVERING FOOD TO HIM.

Panel 8:

IT'S ALREADY PAST HIS FEEDING TIME SO YOU'D BETTER HURRY WITH THAT PIZZA...

UM...OKAY. WHICH OFFICE?

Panel 9:

GRRRRROOOWWWWWWLLLL

YE **GODS**, WAS THAT HIS **STOMACH**?!

OH NO... THAT WAS **HIM**.

GEEK RANT

HI...

I DON'T WEAR BAD GLASSES OR SUSPENDERS AND I DON'T GLOW IN THE DARK.

I DON'T LIKE POCKET PROTECTORS AND NO, I DON'T KNOW EDWIN, MARTY OR LINDA IN THE I.T. DEPARTMENT AT *EBAY*, ALTHOUGH I'M CERTAIN THEY'RE PULLING DOWN GREAT SALARIES...

I LIKE CAFFEINE. I PREFER TO CODE IN *C* OR *PERL*, NOT VISUAL BASIC, AND IT'S PRONOUNCED *LI*-NIX, *LINE*-UX OR *LEEN*-OOKS, WHATEVER MAKES YOU HAPPY.

I CAN PROUDLY WEAR A *T-SHIRT* FROM ANOTHER COMPANY AND STILL LOOK COOL.

I BELIEVE IN INNOVATION, *NOT* OBFUSCATION; PEER REVIEW, *NOT* PATENT WARS, AND THAT THE PENGUIN IS A CUTE BUT FEARSOME ANIMAL!

GEEKS ARE THE *SECOND* BEST PAID PEOPLE IN THE WORLD, THE *FIRST* TO BE BLAMED FOR TECHNICAL PROBLEMS, AND THE *ONLY* REASON WHY CIVILIZATION DOESN'T CRUMBLE AROUND YOUR EARS!

MY NAME IS JASON, AND I AM A GEEK!

65

AFTER MISSING LONDON LINUX EXPO DUE TO FOOD POISONING, ILLIAD IS "PROTECTED" BY DARK SIDE DAVE WHEN ILLIAD EXPRESSES A DESIRE TO GO ROLLERBLADING JUST BEFORE THE TRIP TO LINUXTAG.

68

GEEK IN A CAN

DIRECTIONS: POINT NOZZLE AT TECHNICAL PROBLEM AND SPRAY, HOLDING DOWN BUTTON UNTIL CAN IS EMPTY AND GEEK HAS FORMED. GEEK WILL BEGIN SOLVING PROBLEM AND WILL NOT STOP UNTIL SOLUTION HAS BEEN DEVISED. IF GRUNTING OR RUMBLING NOISES ISSUE FORTH FROM GEEK, POUR EQUAL PARTS SALT, SUGAR, STARCH AND CAFFEINE INTO MOST AVAILABLE ORIFICE.

ONCE PROBLEM HAS BEEN SOLVED, *DO NOT ENTERTAIN GEEK*. GEEK WILL ONLY LEAVE WHEN BORED. SPEAK TO GEEK AND YOU MAY AS WELL PREPARE TO HAVE A HOUSEGUEST FOR THE NEXT DECADE,

COMES IN BOTH MALE AND FEMALE FLAVOURS. BOTH GENDERS ARE EQUALLY COMPETENT, HOWEVER MIXING THEM MAY LEAD TO STRANGE BEHAVIOURS IN MALE GEEKS.

71

SPY VS. SPY VS. CONSUMER

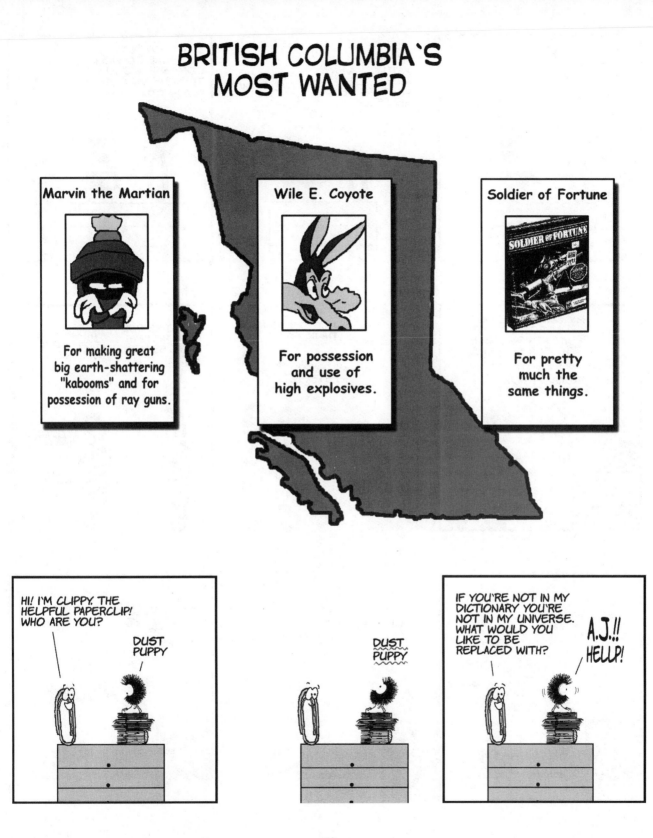

OBSOLESCENCE
IN THE MUSIC INDUSTRY

REEL-TO-REEL TAPE

8-TRACK TAPE

VINYL LPS

MAJOR
RECORD
LABELS

81

BRITISH GOVERNMENT OPERATIONS MANUAL

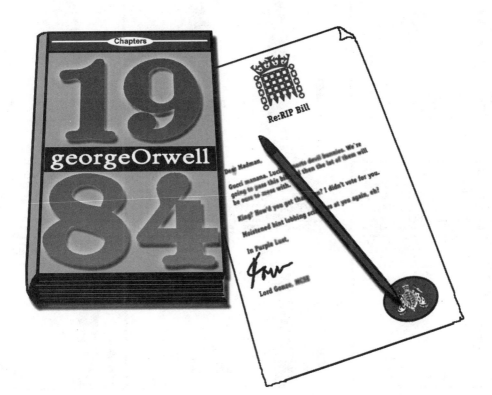

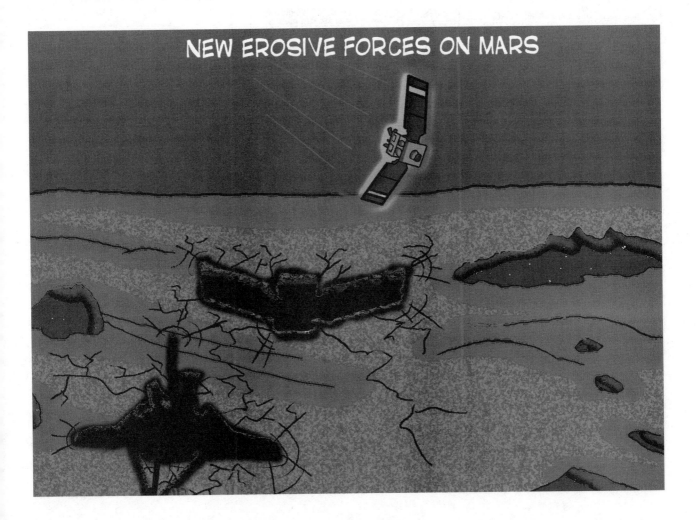

NEW EROSIVE FORCES ON MARS

SONY DEVELOPS TECHNOLOGY
THAT TRANCENDS THE INDIVIDUAL USER

95

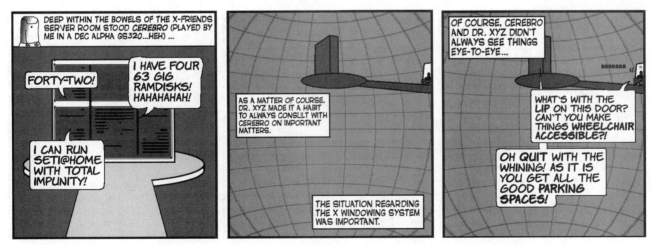

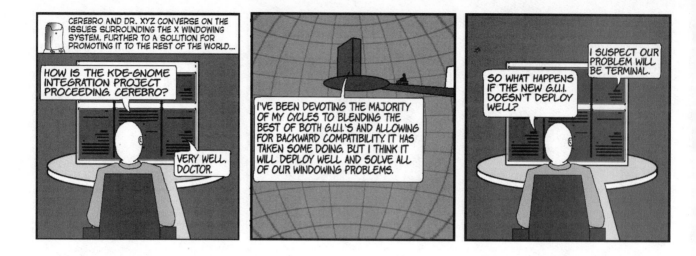

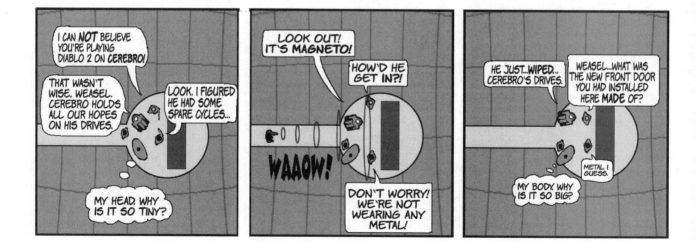

IN THE SPIRIT OF SYDNEY 2000
INTEL EXECUTIVES ATTEMPT TO
ADOPT THE OLYMPIC SLOGAN

TECHIE CAREER TRACK FLOWCHART

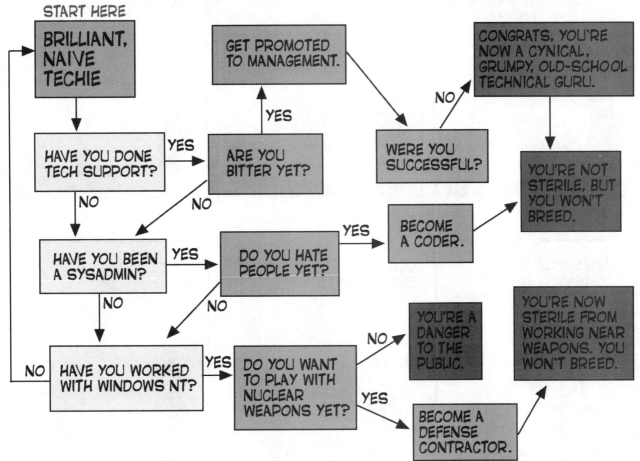

UNFORTUNATE LOGO DESIGN #14:

"MISTAKEN FOR A DEVICE IN A PROCTOLOGIST'S OFFICE"

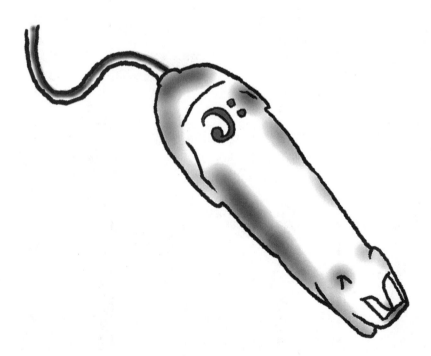

108

ONE-CLICK SPAM BLOCKING

SID? WHY IS PITR FUMING?

PROBABLY BECAUSE I GAVE HIM AN INTELLECTUAL MANBEATING AGAIN.

YOU KNOW SID, PITR'S NOT SOMEONE YOU WANT TO GET TOO EXCITED. HE'S ALREADY GOT A POOR GRIP ON REALITY AS IT IS AND IF YOU PUSH HIM OVER THE EDGE HE COULD SNAP AND GO QUASI-DIMENSIONAL ON US.

I UNDERSTAND. THANK YOU.

GOOD. SO DOES THAT MEAN YOU'RE GOING TO APOLOGIZE TO HIM?

HELL NO. I'M GOING TO PLAY WITH HIS MIND SOME MORE. WANT TO HELP?

COME ON. HELP ME PLAY A PRANK ON PITR...

SID. YOU DON'T KNOW WHAT YOU'RE ASKING HERE...

LOOK. YOU'RE ASKING ME TO BETRAY A LONG-TIME CO-WORKER. WE'VE BEEN THROUGH A LOT TOGETHER. AND DESPITE HIS EXTREME MOODS AND HIS OVERALL SELFISH DEMEANOR, NOT TO MENTION HIS "I'M BETTER THAN YOU" ATTITUDE OR HIS...UM...HIS...UHH...

UM...WHY AM I NOT HELPING YOU AGAIN?

AHHH. YOU MUST HAVE JUST ENTERED MID-LIFE. ISN'T IT COOL HOW TREACHERY JUST SEEMS RIGHT?

WELCOME TO MATURITY, MIKE. YOU'VE OFFICIALLY GROWN UP.

THANKS. I THINK.

OH DON'T DOUBT YOURSELF! YOU'RE NOW AT THE POINT IN YOUR LIFE WHERE YOU CAN LOOK BACK AND SMILE AT YOUR ACCOMPLISHMENTS, WATCH THE YOUNG ONES FLAIL AROUND IN THEIR MEDIOCRITY, AND SIT BACK KNOWING THAT YOU'VE MADE IT.

I'M ABOUT TO DIE. AREN'T I.

HECK NO. IT MEANS YOU CAN WRITE BAD CODE AND PEOPLE WILL JUST CALL IT "OBFUSCATED!"

IN ONE FELL SWOOP, SANTA DECIDES EVERYONE
IS NAUGHTY THIS YEAR AND PROCEEDS TO PLAN
OUT HIS RETIREMENT ON EBAY.

129